Head Injury: Pros and Cons

M. Renae Dubois

Acknowledgement of Country

I acknowledge the Traditional Custodians of the land on which this work was written and created, the Turrbal and Yugara peoples of Meanjin, and I pay my deep respects to their Elders, past, present, and emerging.

I honour their unbroken connection to land, language, story, and culture, and recognise that sovereignty was never ceded.

I extend this respect to all First Nations peoples across Australia, whose voices, histories, and creative traditions continue to guide and enrich this place.

Contents

Introduction 5
Welcome 6
Ode to Koffies 1
Beginning..2
Claret 3
Beginnings 4
Slutski 5
Mrs Fields Cookies 6
Fortitude Valley...7
Ladies..9
Journal #11 11
"I'm working" 12
Sydney Bound.. 13
Glamour.. 15
Sydney is down 17
Sydney 19
Coming back 20
Wuss 21
Brisbane Again 22
Des 23
Me 24
Lighting 25
Whole Truth 26
June 27
Accident Tales 28
Weakday 29
Angrily 31
Jason... 32
Astronaut 33
Current Form.. 35
Decisions and Delusions 36

Raid	37
Confront	39
Promises	40
So I'm lonely	41
Damaged In Pain	42
Wacol	43
Deszy	45
Oh No!	46
Mum and Me	47
The Base Element	48
Penny Fuck	49
A-Ha!	50
Working Life	51
Tricks of the Trade	52
Wake up Call	53
Cycle starts again	54
No	55
I'm back	56
Disordered Workers Life	57
Conviction or Convicted	59
Epiphany	61
The Endurance of It	62
Epilogue	63
Abortion	64
A Grief	66
My Manifesto	68

Introduction

This work is the revised and improved upon version of my first novel, Curses of Verses: A Head Injury Tale. The initial manuscript had been resting in my bedside drawer for close to 20 years, before it was rescued during the Covid pandemic of 2020, when I had other reasons for being unwell.

In the process of publishing and marketing it, a clarity began to form, and a direction took shape. I have since embarked on a mission of education and literary nourishment, and written two more verse-novels in this series.

I see this book as a time capsule from a period of my life influenced by youth, brain injury, undirected intelligence, and desire.

This version includes new work, that will go some way to explaining certain endings, as well as some corrections, both in form and style.

It is worth noting that I have changed the name of at least one of the characters.

Please enjoy, and look out for the other books in the series:- Utterly: a Biography in Verse, and Coy Candour. 2025

Welcome

Traumatic Brain Injury can have many difficult and different symptoms, physical and psychological. Risk-taking, substance abuse, memory problems, hypersexuality, and an altered state of consciousness are common psychological symptoms. This book is a partly fictionalized portrayal of some of these such processes. I began writing within months of leaving hospital in 1991 at the age of 16.
2020

Ode to Koffies

The clatter of the combination
Of cafe crowd and coffee espresso
Kept a continuous cacophony
Of controlled chaos.

The populace of particulars
Postured pretentiously,
Playing at the picture of
Post-pubescent parody.

Simmering, my spirit
Stung in the symphony as
Suspicion and scorn
Swelled in my soul.

Beginning

I had a major head injury,
A coma for a week
I was driving with a family friend
Hit a truck on narrow street

Now I've left my high school
I've got a job as well
But I can't control my wayward mouth
And my burning inner swell

Claret

As I sit with glass in front of me,
I am inclined to think
Of all that lies ahead of me
Including this foul drink

I'd like to be an artist
But I am no good at art
I'd like to be a composer
Cause music's in my heart

Talentless, I feel I am
I don't know where to go
Working retail, selling shoes
Looking people in the toe

Do I want to drink this stuff?
Is wine my vice to be?
An artist suffers everyday
Can see that will be me

But whats my music I don't know
Whats my favourite kind of art?
Oh hell, too hard, I think Ill go and
Have a drink and be a tart

Beginnings

I suppose you want to know about me
Who I really am,
I'll tell you more as you go on
Of where I all began

Now to suffice – I'm seventeen
A virgin only just
Left school after knock on head
Giving everyone my trust

There is a magic innocence
It has a witch-like stare
It's complex and confusing
Not appealing so to bare

For now read on, you'll discover more
Of where I found to go
I'll give you hints – there's a word in there
That rhymes with lo, roe, joe, woah, foe

Slutski

The guy I did the other day
Found me stumbling up the mall
He left the girl he'd cornered there
A chat-up he would take the fall

To take me to a nightclub
Buy me another drink
I didn't even want one
But didn't choose to think

Since then I've done a bouncer
A streetie, and a yob
I'm losing touch with feeling
But it's easy to please a nob

Mrs Fields Cookies

"Hereya, have three"
"Of these Brownies, you're sure?"
"Yeah take them you're hungry
Do you want some more?"

"No, wow so good of you,
What time do you close?"
"We close when the centre shuts
Then I hit the road"

"To home you mean?"
"Well yeah for a while
But only so I can change
And go out in style"

"Where do you go?"
"To raves and the Beat.
They once had a slippery dip
And spa for your feet!"

"I'll have to go check this out
What is your name?"
"You can call me on this number
And Jason's my name."

Fortitude Valley

The valley is full of
Crusties and nerds
They all are escaping
From the city herd

But to escape in the valley?
Still, it's a thrill
And I'm here, so there you go
I know the will

The source of enjoyment
In being yourself

The valley forces you
To work it, to hell

With the rest
What do they know?
We all are in limbo
And in the flow

Strut it, Work it
Show us your stuff
If you think you're so good
Then smooth over the rough

Do you have something
That exceeds the rest?
I believe you, no really!
But I'm still the best

At least in my own mind
And that's where it lies
The panic of initiation
Mutates into thrive

And once you have got it
Don't ever give in
Cause you can take it
Wherever you sin.

Ladies

Pretty features
Muted clothes
The talk is chirping
Not overblown

The excitement accentuated
By gurgling slurs
The voices intermingle
The words unheard

A quiet descends
And tension is sensed
The girls don't like anyone
Who's too intense

Mistress of madness
Sitting alone
The latte growing colder
The cigarette blown

Fairy lights
Jingle stills
Coffee crowd
And crystal bells

Ladies make the
Night light flow
In happy enchantment
The magic shows.

The magic is broken
A guest has spoken
"Hey Hey its Saturday"
Destroys any token

Of sophisticated company
And class in style
The media impact
Has not raised a smile

Luckily the waitress
Intervenes on time
And those who know better
Find a new rhyme.

Journal #11

It makes sense to make a go of
Prostitution for a change
I'm fucking all these idiots
I may as well make some real gains

Golden Girls or VIP
Doesn't matter – all the same
I did a night - it worked out well
I get there on the train

Five days down, still no regrets
Expecting it to get better yet
I'll work from Sydney, yeah, I know!
I'll find a parlour and a flat to let

No one should know that I'm leaving
No one would like me to go
I'll have to take that dingy car
Get to Sydney, be a ho.

"I'm working"

"I started, Jay
I started the job
Seven hundred dollars down
It's no fucking slog

Yes, I do females too
No I don't spank
Well not as a permanent thing
Just as a wank

Jay stop all this bullshit
When you gonna start
You told me we'd do it
Put it into my heart

Whatever you are gonna do
I'm having a good time
It doesn't seem disgusting
Nor like a warning sign

Sydney Bound

I stole that car – my boyfriend's car
The one I got my license on
A Torana, red is what I've got
To get to Sydney, on the run

It's Byron Bay, there's people here
Who want to come with me down south
They can drive my car, and share the load
And who knows, they might even shout

Arduous this journey is
And in this car it's not real safe
Coffs Harbour now; I wonder how
Long it's gonna take

Aah, we made it here, I see the bridge
Let's cross it now, and seal our night
If we just choose the right lane - oh shit
What was the fucking point?

A bloody tunnel - great
What a style to start the stay
Misdirection; under the bridge
Why is this always my way?

Stay positive; stay upbeat now
It won't do to get depressed
This is a big progression and
You can't afford to fail the test

Glamour

Terrace house
Decked to the hilt
There's no hint of trash
In the curtains of silk

This is what I knew
Sydney was for
A sex workers paradise
Open for all

I'm loving the sex
Loved to be slut!
But there's no money in fucking around
Free sex is a stupid rut

I like their machismo
Although most men are foul
But their easier than women
Who are smart and cruel

So I've become a hermit
If you can call it that
I stay in my beautiful parlour
And fuck them till they're flat

I fuck them hard; I make them work
At the moment I'm on my back
But when they're gone I get a thrill
And add money to the stack

Of things that God has given me
Just for being alive
In this sordid industry
My twisted ego thrives.

Sydney is down

"There you go, you fucking slut
Rub that on your gums
Cocaine will see what you have got"
Or if it's you that I will shun.

"Not that way, bitch - stupid slut,
Why don't you get a life?
I'm paying for your drugs right here
You're gonna get me into strife."

"I didn't actually want this
I wasn't in the mood
You got me at a real bad time
I wasn't ready, dude"

"We're going for a walk right now,
Why don't you come along"
Stumbling, I followed after them
In a daze I brought the bong

I shudder now to think of it
How messy that all was,
Some fucking bitch got me with that shit
She was too high to give a toss

Right in my lounge room,
Right after work,
I'd had a bad day as it was
I didn't need this jerk

Sydney

Platforms and fishnets
Mascara and mini
My hair was dishevelled
My eyes were spinning

In 10.30 glare
On Wednesday morning
All I wanted was coffee
To stop me yawning

No kettle at home
The thought pissed me off
I walked into Chandlers
And gave a loud cough

"Show me your kettles"
"I want the best"
Brashly and rudely
Fuck the rest.

Coming back

They tell me I should go back
I'm not convinced they're wrong
I'm toying with some scary thoughts
But I haven't been here long

The parlour where I'm working
Is new and really slow
I don't like staying every day
And not bringing in the dough

I need to change my image
I need to move my stuff
I want to be free in a space
Without acting really tough

I want to lose a bit more weight
I want to tone it up
I want to park my car at work
Without getting a ticket stub

I've got these pills - they're Mersyndols
I got two packets to decide
Will I take them all at once
And exit with the tide?

Wuss

"A Bipolar, a Borderline"
"You'll be treated for them now on in.
Medication is what you'll get
And hospital when you're misbehaving"

I feel I should explain myself
Who I am and what I know
This is why I am myself
This is what I feel I know

They tell me my good sense is gone
And that my brain doesn't function right
They've shoved me in a corner
And I don't want to fight

So I'll take my choice of drugs thank you
And I hope I don't get caught
Trial procedures bad enough
The psychiatrists have already wrought...

No, they'll send me to hospital
And tear apart my brain
Peeling off the layers until
They find a conducive vein

Brisbane Again

They got me back -it's not so bad
I'm living with a friend
I've got some sexy pieces
Oblivious to trend

The hairstyle's long and then it's short
The colour changes too
I'm spending all my money
Just to get a new hairdo

I don't know where to start to work
I can't here at my friends
I think I'll go into the mall
See if I can meet some men

I'm thinking hard but errantly
About what I can do next
I'm looking for a dealer though
And I sent someone a text

Des

I found a lovely man today
That I've been looking for, for years
I used to know him averagely
But his absence caused no tears

The most professional man I've met
He definitely knows the score
Aware of his face, knows his place
And doesn't ask for more

We're acting on our instincts
And going with the flow
The flow is good
And we both know.

Me

He mentioned sex quite easily
My God we have done well
But I'm a worker so I can't
Just relieve his primal swell

I know he doesn't let himself
Go through with sex at all
But he knew that I wanted it
So he must trust me or he'd stall

I told him that I couldn't sleep
With anyone for free
I told him how that went against
My entire morality

It was the truth - a vow I'd made
Before he came back on my scene
So many people just don't accept
What sex can really mean

Now I feel I'm getting more
Of everything that I want most
This guy's for real, when he sleeps with me
He always puts me first.

Lighting

His passion for history
Moves me deeply
Antiques in his home
Restore the past eerily

A railway clock keeps that time
And these items there
A picture of Queen Vic
And her dogged stare

Couch is leather,
Lamps abound
Every evening at six
Lighting changes round

No more a balcony
With back yard views
Rather tall curtains,
And golden hues

This life is a dream,
The aroma the best
I love my new life
With Des and the rest

Whole Truth

Our relationship is better
Than how it started out
Both of us are talking now
Love and what that's about

That's what we talk about
When we're in bed
Most of the time we're
In each others head

He is in my vision
Every minute of the day
And I know he is watching me
In the same way

Assessing each others images
And how we relate to some
We've gotten a little egotistic
But that is part of the fun

We know we're good people
He says we're the best
We couldn't be though
If you know the rest

June

How do I love
This man of my dreams
He's everything I wanted
It's mutual it seems

But that is a crazy
Illusion of mine
I couldn't be really
The sign of his times

I'm just a girlfriend
And he is my lover
He does what he does
I don't play big brother

To love him I let him
Decide for himself
Although the return of that favour
Is not mutually felt

I don't understand
What he's trying to do
"You said that you wanted
A woman to fit into you!"

Accident Tales

Fuck fuck fuck fuck fuck fuck fuck
I feel like such a jerk
I'm with a loved one in my life
But I still feel I'm in search

In search for stable peace of mind
And what that myth might mean
I think it means that I can handle
Any sort of scene

Head injury at seventeen
A compo battle now
I can't get away from all
The medico-legal rows

The lawyers have taken away my right
To fuck up on my own
The years from which I've learnt the most
Have been spoiled from early on.

Their words, reports and worse
The thought, I cannot write a will
Have driven home their cruelty
In present, past and future still.

Weakday

This morning my feelings
Were confused

My head was dizzy
And my body felt tired

I could not sleep
I did not know what

I wanted to do

So I had a cup of tea
and slept

Within the blanket of
open eyes

My dressing gown did
fall apart

And in a wave my head
fell back

Clunk

Against the wall.

Slowly the eventualness
Pattered at my consciousness
Grinding at my layers
Carving out my soul

Perspective regained in my mind
Gently though at least
A point of view is special
It's all my territory

Only my eyes count for much
It is my brain after all
The truth does slip into place
And now it's my call.

Angrily

I gave up the sex work
Threw myself into you
Not asking for anything
Except something to do

We see my writing
Get better in style
So I cling on to what
Will cause inspiration to rile

But like any artist
(Bored housewife too)
I've been taking narcotics
Not unlike you

I've got my aggression
I can feel the strength grow
Confidence and assertiveness
But I actually know

That I have a habit
Amphetamine time
I'm not feeling bad about it
I'm enjoying my rhyme.

Jason

I've got to get a grip on it
You've got to understand
This is a whole new life for me
I don't want to hold your hand

Jay you think I am a pro
That that is who I am
You've lost the plot and gone all weird
You're strange in your demands

I'm giving up on you my friend
You are not what I need
I need to be a woman now
I don't want to fit your creed

Astronaut

My thoughts are skimming past the surface
Of a romantic dream
In the midst of the confusion
My body followed steam

I am forced to take a step back
And to open up my eyes
In my brain there is a mission
That's what he sees inside

A girl of ambition
Who cannot sit still
It is a fusion
Of body and will

But the trust of my partner
Has become paramount
Have I been looking for someone
To believe in my stunt?

I know I can do it
I believe in my strength
And God, what a struggle
For mental health

I told him about myself
Needing some space
I told him about writing
And getting out of his face

But, no more justifications
A fact is a fact
I shall be leaving this house soon
And getting a flat.

Current Form

Holding back on friendliness
Bringing in the sign
I feel so unattractive though
If I don't pay them for their time

I find though when I pull back
And stay in my own zone
That things can work out perfectly
And in a pleasant tone

I'm a bad girl
And playing at being weak
And alone is not necessary
My boyfriend knows

I am not "spreading my oats"
as he said.
"I already have a crop"
That's what I said

Decisions and Delusions

We did the deed together
We did it really well
We found the perfect home for me
It's mine and we can tell

Art deco style
With plastered ceilings
The rooms are furnished
There's a labyrinthic feeling

It's my little mansion
All I need is, well, everything
But Deszy helped me pay for it
So I'll get the rest through my thing

I don't know how yet
But I feel like a scammer
Maybe I've always been
At least I'm not on the hammer

Raid

I awoke on Saturday afternoon
Naked on Des' bed
He was wandering in and out of there
Clearly using his head

I noticed lots of bags around
The type for Des' bits
His mate, who lived with him as well
Was busy doing sticks

Des came back into the room
And gave me some good news
There was some smack and speed on its way
All for him and me to use

At the door there was a knock
Which Davo went to answer
The cops are here, he ran back to say
And grabbed two bags of hydro

I pulled the sheets to thinly disguise
That I was a naked female
My hair was a mess and I must confess
I chose to play the detail

I must be naïve, because an hour ago
I thought they'd let him come home
But I figure that now he's in the watchouse in town
And they won't let him go near the phone

Confront

He's gone away
Just like that
I cannot hide today

Or any day, I have to do
What's right by him and me
I've got to put a brave face on
Until to the woods I flee

I love him, yes truly
But what are we facing?
Six months, six years
Is the law faking?

He is getting punished
I'm not to share
If I am miserable
He will not care

No I have to be stronger
Than I've ever been
And I'm already failing
And being seen.

Promises

Promised I was worth it
Told that I deserved it
Compensation was put to me
As a reason for how I be

Pain, yeah I'm hurting
Miserable suicidal madness
Is it because of
My head injury?

Sold my soul
Is reality
I sold my belief in myself
For compo money

They've given me false hope in legality
They're not on my side
Psychiatry?

So I'm lonely

I missed your call for fifty bucks
This proves to me that my life sucks

Damaged In Pain

They are low down dirty cunts
I told you so before
This age is now self-seeking, so
There is room for my raw sore

I will let speed enliven my soul
And it's true that it is hard
To remember who you really are
With a needle up your arm

Wacol

The sun on my legs is
Burning warm
The glare from the page
The eye of the storm

There's the mentals, indigenous
The elderly, the kids
The bush bandits, the crusties
And the old man who spits

There's a postbox and a Cornetto sign
An overpass and a fence
The railway passes through here
The station is intense

Two general convenience stores
That cater for everyone
The food is semi-edible
But sitting here is fun

I have to wait for twelve you see
To get into the local jail
You know that this is Wacol
And my boyfriend didn't get bail

I have to let them play their game
And we have to follow the system
For what he did they have to push
His head into the cistern

They've got a job to do
And regulations to abide
Des is cut off from the real world
And doesn't feel the tide

He shouldn't feel the tide as such
That's what he's in there for
An extradition from the external world
Life in there must be a bore

Deszy

I don't know what we said today yet
Because I'm waiting to go in
As you know I came this morning
But they wouldn't let me in

I was a little late my love
I hope you weren't distressed
Everything I try to do these days
Turns out a miserable mess

I'm working all the details out
And sorting out your stuff
But people out here think I'm mad
So it is really tough

Not to load all that on you
The worst part about being mad
Is that straight people magnify the detail
And treat me really bad

Still, it's good for me, that attitude
It's time I toughened up
Having you in there and me out here
Had better lead to moving up

Oh No!

The concept of living
To protect my arse
Doesn't seem so bad now
If that's the ask

I'm pretty self-seeking
That's the clue
The realisation is unshocking
They are too

Yeah I'll join your fight
For my right
To be myself
My mouth shut tight

But I can't do that
I know it
So I'll talk in different melody
Same old shit

No emotion, no bare souls
No room for broken hearts
Honesty in untruthfulness
Will take me further fast

Mum and Me

I'm getting really mental Mum
I think I'm going mad
I'm not sure of the time of day
And my life is really bad

Please come and do the washing
I can't stand to look once more at it
The smell is bad, I can't eat in here
Everything's covered in cocky shit

And while you're here you can help me
With the things I've gotta do
Don't answer back. I know I'm right
Why do you create a major coup?

I feel you're getting down on me
I think you're really pissed
But I don't care if you feel that way
Cause I want to be the bitch

Dad, it happened again, she got my goat,
Please tell her of my side
I can't handle all the bullshit
When I'm living to survive

The Base Element

For all of the bullshit, the whoring can stay
I don't know why I do it, is it really the pay?
It's not for the sex or the feel of male sweat
And it's definitely not 'cause I'm horny and wet
People I take one-on-one now you see?
It's easier. A cop-out? Perhaps, but fuck me!

Penny Fuck

Going so low is lethal
My ad is very cheap
It's not even in my area
I'm meeting some real creeps

I'm going to get off 'action' drugs
I'm going to stick with pot
I'm going to get away from this
Stupid fucking lot

I'll look for a brothel
A small little place
But busy, must be busy
Get me back in the race

A-Ha!

I'm working in a brothel
A clean and quiet place
The girls are good but bitchy
So I try to set my pace

We compete for their attention
The customers I mean
One by one we all go out
And return, grimacing

Everybody's desperate
We badly need to earn
I much preferred being on my own
Than taking fucking turn

Working Life

What is this? An intro?
Oh God I hate this shit
The politics of who wins the job
And then the whispers, "Bitch"

Some hang around, cajoling
Some make it very fast
We all are on our tenterhooks
"Please make this traffic last"

I think they want a female
Who can get down on the floor
Get completely dirty
And smile through it all

Take it now, and take it all
I grimace and oblige
It's all for one and all for me
For both on either side

Tricks of the Trade

"Get off your back and on your knees,
It's better for your bum"
I felt guilty then because I knew
How idle I had been for some

"The main thing is make them happy
Give them what they want
Don't put up with shit but give a bit
Show them what you've got"

No time to work out? Work out on them
Be discreet though if you're worried
Men will believe you look alright
If you don't let on you're bothered

Wake up Call

My pills aren't working
Confusing at least
They worked so well
That I thought that was it

A few years go by
Addiction in place
To these pills that aren't working
And my public face

Is down the plug hole
And out the door
I've been losing the plot
For three years or more

Cycle starts again

I have to keep on working
I'll change the meds for sure
But working suits me like it or not
I'll advertise even more

My thoughts are 'get my meds right'
and find an even balance
Then I will be working even harder
And using my business talents

No

Women are women
And sex workers are too
To work in the industry
I need a view

Perspective that stops me
From feeling raped
I have to know that I am right
Or I'd know that I am bait

It has just meant that I've been used
In every different way
Sometimes I don't know how to act
I feel that I should play

Whenever someone's nice to me
I feel I owe them some
I don't have much to give though, now
Except the tales that I can spin

They only like to hear my tales
Because it reinforces their idea
That I like the image I've created
And I sometimes live in fear.

I'm back

I'm working from my own place now
They come in through the front
I'm not ashamed; nothing to hide
If neighbours ask I'm blunt

The ad is good; the clients great
I'm really pulling in
I look real good from loss in weight
But not everyone likes me thin

For now I've got the flat I want
Paying often and steady rent
I'm earning all the cash I need
And refrain from getting bent

The main point is I'm legal
On my own and very straight
I've got everything I could really want
I don't need a constant mate.

Disordered Workers Life

Bipolar disorder makes this job easy
For me, and a pleasure to do
It helps me to beat the
Illness and teaches me too

First there's the phone calls
My response changes each time
In the early days nothing is sure
I'll work out my line

Then they arrive
Crucial this moment
It determines the drive
Makes it easy to hone it

Intros are different for everyone
And unique for me
Do they reject me,
And curse as they leave?

When I am lucky,
And they stay for the hour
After is hard times
Having cash can turn sour

I used to get manic
Go out and spend
Now I wait longer
And no longer pretend

That it will not affect me
It does and it will
So these days I clean more
Before counting the till

Conviction or Convicted

I found a piece of paper
Hidden in a book
The message was a real one
I took a closer look

The words that Des had written
Deserved an explanation fast
"You are not a man of conviction
You only think you are"

Later on he told me
That it was written to
A temporary mate who'd told him
How his past was true

I think that when I look back
I could say the very same
It's unreasonable to think other
Since I am not so . . . tame

A smart head on young shoulders
Has the desired effect
Of justifying anything
Tomorrow to affect

And affect the situation
Is exactly what we do
When we easily make decisions
And then follow through

Epiphany

I wish I didn't get angry
I wish I didn't get loud
I wish I could say I didn't put up with this shit
Without voicing my concerns out so loud.
The truth is I did get real angry
I lost the plot time and again
But I was raging against the wrong people I think
And it's a bad habit I still attend
The ones who should have been angering me
Were the ones who were sticking it in
But I felt like they understood me
In some bent way, but not like my kin
My mother calls me a pervert
My brother doesn't call me at all
They don't understand; they think that's my fault
Like from my stance I should naturally fall
I just wish I'd been taught so much sooner
Taught respectful, mutual love
Coz I took their mistrust and derision
And gave myself up for a buck.

The Endurance of It

I remember all the people
Who felt I wasn't worth
The effort they had made with me
Their departures made things worse
It wasn't til there was no one left
That I started to get well
But that was just the end result
The path to which was hell
My mental health was always on
The table with my peers
It was always the excuse for
Bad behavior through the years
But maybe mental illness
For me was just a ruse
I also tried to use it
As a profitable excuse
These days I am wholly sick
Of defining myself that way
I'm sick of acting sick
But it will not go away

Epilogue

The following two poems were too difficult to write for many years, and it has taken a half a lifetime of self-reflection and seeking personal insight, that I permitted myself to explore this difficult time. Even so, there are details in these poems, as in the rest of the book, which are not intended to be indicative of actual events, or their justifications.

Abortion

He's leaving me barren, aborted at the source,
He exited prison so healthy, I got pregnant yes of course.
We never used protection, it was silly as all hell,
I've been working my little ass off while he's been in a cell.
I used them with my clients but not in my private life to date
And now my period is due, and it is all too late.
I cannot go through birth, it seems like utter torture
And I wouldn't want to give the bub to Mum, I think she'd hurt her
I cannot have a child like this, living week to week,
Shacked up with a dealer who can't his ends make meet.
I'm using speed while pregnant and yes I am ashamed
But addicted and unmedicated so maybe not to blame.
We've broken up, I mean, obviously, this whole thing's way too bad

And now I'm thinking way too much and I am very sad

A Grief

Acceptance of an apology
That's all I had to do
The broken man who fronted
For the things he did, he rued

Not long emancipated
Let out of the cell
To come home to loving girlfriend
To find herself she'd sell

I wrapped him in addiction
That I'd continued on
While he was being punished
For his strictly legal wrong

So we'd fought in our drug stupor
We'd yelled and even struck
He's gone out to get some heroin
And now was feeling yuck

So proud of getting clean in jail
But now to see his slut
Carry on and bait him
He slams the front door shut

And I am left now reeling
It will take years for me to see
How shockingly I treated him
And where that would leave me

Broke, with pregnant belly
No more home to rent
Back with my own parents
My liberty's been spent

My Manifesto

Positivity is the answer
A filter for the pain
Chaotic life or no, my dear
The pain is there the same

Accept the truth, hold on to it
You have a reason to be sad
Let that be a source of strength
Not an excuse for bad

Find a way to build a bridge
Walk across the filthy muck
Don't let people get you down
And give a pleasant fuck.

www.ingramcontent.com/pod-product-compliance
Lightning Source LLC
Chambersburg PA
CBHW062121080426
42734CB00012B/2937